jazz stand

Arranged by Brent Edstrom

contents

2　ALONE TOGETHER

6　APRIL IN PARIS ✓

12　HAVE YOU MET MISS JONES? ✓

16　HOW HIGH THE MOON ✓

9　I CAN'T GET STARTED ✓

20　I COVER THE WATERFRONT

23　I'LL REMEMBER APRIL

28　ISN'T IT ROMANTIC?

33　IT COULD HAPPEN TO YOU ✓

38　JUST FRIENDS

43　LOVER MAN (OH, WHERE CAN YOU BE?)

46　MEAN TO ME ✓

54　OUT OF NOWHERE

58　THE SONG IS YOU

49　STOMPIN' AT THE SAVOY

62　SWEET GEORGIA BROWN

67　THERE IS NO GREATER LOVE

72　THERE WILL NEVER BE ANOTHER YOU ✓

78　WHEN SUNNY GETS BLUE

82　YESTERDAYS

88　YOU DON'T KNOW WHAT LOVE IS

92　YOU STEPPED OUT OF A DREAM

ISBN 978-1-4950-6552-1

HAL•LEONARD®
7777 W. BLUEMOUND RD. P.O. BOX 13819 MILWAUKEE, WI 53213

Visit Hal Leonard Online at
www.halleonard.com

ALONE TOGETHER

Lyrics by HOWARD DIET
Music by ARTHUR SCHWART

4

APRIL IN PARIS

Words by E.Y. "YIP" HARBURG
Music by VERNON DUKE

Freely, straight 8ths

I CAN'T GET STARTED

from ZIEGFELD FOLLIES

Words by IRA GERSHWIN
Music by VERNON DUKE

HAVE YOU MET MISS JONES?

from I'D RATHER BE RIGHT

Words by LORENZ HART
Music by RICHARD RODGERS

HOW HIGH THE MOON
from TWO FOR THE SHOW

Lyrics by NANCY HAMILTON
Music by MORGAN LEWIS

19

I COVER THE WATERFRONT

Words by EDWARD HEYMAN
Music by JOHNNY GREEN

I'LL REMEMBER APRIL

Words and Music by PAT JOHNSTON,
DON RAYE and GENE DE PAUL

In the style of Erroll Garner

ISN'T IT ROMANTIC?

from the Paramount Picture LOVE ME TONIGHT

Words by LORENZ HART
Music by RICHARD RODGERS

IT COULD HAPPEN TO YOU

from the Paramount Picture AND THE ANGELS SING

Words by JOHNNY BURKE
Music by JAMES VAN HEUSEN

JUST FRIENDS

Lyrics by SAM M. LEWIS
Music by JOHN KLENNER

LOVER MAN
(Oh, Where Can You Be?)

Words and Music by JIMMY DAVIS,
ROGER RAMIREZ and JIMMY SHERMAN

MEAN TO ME

Lyric by ROY TURK
Music by FRED E. AHLERT

STOMPIN' AT THE SAVOY

By BENNY GOODMAN,
EDGAR SAMPSON and CHICK WEBB

Bright Swing

OUT OF NOWHERE
from the Paramount Picture DUDE RANCH

Words by EDWARD HEYMAN
Music by JOHNNY GREEN

THE SONG IS YOU
from MUSIC IN THE AIR

Lyrics by OSCAR HAMMERSTEIN II
Music by JEROME KERN

SWEET GEORGIA BROWN

Words and Music by BEN BERNIE,
MACEO PINKARD and KENNETH CASEY

66

THERE IS NO GREATER LOVE

Words by MARTY SYMES
Music by ISHAM JONES

To Coda

THERE WILL NEVER BE ANOTHER YOU

from the Motion Picture ICELAND

Lyric by MACK GORDON
Music by HARRY WARREN

WHEN SUNNY GETS BLUE

Lyric by JACK SEGAL
Music by MARVIN FISHER

80

YESTERDAYS
from ROBERTA

Words by OTTO HARBACH
Music by JEROME KERN

84

YOU DON'T KNOW WHAT LOVE IS

Words and Music by DON RAYE
and GENE DE PAUL

YOU STEPPED OUT OF A DREAM
from the M-G-M Picture ZIEGFELD GIRL

Words by GUS KAHN
Music by NACIO HERB BROWN

The Best-Selling Jazz Book of All Time Is Now Legal!

The Real Books are the most popular jazz books of all time. Since the 1970s, musicians have trusted these volumes to get them through every gig, night after night. The problem is that the books were illegally produced and distributed, without any regard to copyright law, or royalties paid to the composers who created these musical masterpieces.

Hal Leonard is very proud to present the first legitimate and legal editions of these books ever produced. You won't even notice the difference, other than all the notorious errors being fixed: the covers and typeface look the same, the song lists are nearly identical, and the price for our edition is even cheaper than the originals!

Every conscientious musician will appreciate that these books are now produced accurately and ethically, benefitting the songwriters that we owe for some of the greatest tunes of all time!

VOLUME 1
00240221	C Edition	$39.99
00240224	Bb Edition	$39.99
00240225	Eb Edition	$39.99
00240226	Bass Clef Edition	$39.99
00240292	C Edition 6 x 9	$35.00
00240339	Bb Edition 6 x 9	$35.00
00147792	Bass Clef Edition 6 x 9	$35.00
00451087	C Edition on CD-ROM	$29.99
00200984	Online Backing Tracks: Selections	$45.00
00110604	Book/USB Flash Drive Backing Tracks Pack	$79.99
00110599	USB Flash Drive Only	$50.00

VOLUME 2
00240222	C Edition	$39.99
00240227	Bb Edition	$39.99
00240228	Eb Edition	$39.99
00240229	Bass Clef Edition	$39.99
00240293	C Edition 6 x 9	$35.00
00125900	Bb Edition 6 x 9	$35.00
00451088	C Edition on CD-ROM	$30.99
00125900	The Real Book – Mini Edition	$35.00
00204126	Backing Tracks on USB Flash Drive	$50.00
00204131	C Edition – USB Flash Drive Pack	$79.99

VOLUME 3
00240233	C Edition	$39.99
00240284	Bb Edition	$39.99
00240285	Eb Edition	$39.99
00240286	Bass Clef Edition	$39.99
00240338	C Edition 6 x 9	$35.00
00451089	C Edition on CD-ROM	$29.99

VOLUME 4
00240296	C Edition	$39.99
00103348	Bb Edition	$39.99
00103349	Eb Edition	$39.99
00103350	Bass Clef Edition	$39.99

VOLUME 5
00240349	C Edition	$39.99
00175278	Bb Edition	$39.99
00175279	Eb Edition	$39.99

VOLUME 6
00240534	C Edition	$39.99
00223637	Eb Edition	$39.99

Also available:
00154230	The Real Bebop Book	$34.99
00240264	The Real Blues Book	$34.99
00310910	The Real Bluegrass Book	$32.50
00240223	The Real Broadway Book	$35.00
00240440	The Trane Book	$22.99
00125426	The Real Country Book	$39.99
00240355	The Real Dixieland Book C Edition	$32.50
00122335	The Real Dixieland Book Bb Edition	$32.50
00240235	The Duke Ellington Real Book	$19.99
00240268	The Real Jazz Solos Book	$30.00
00240348	The Real Latin Book C Edition	$37.50
00127107	The Real Latin Book Bb Edition	$35.00
00120809	The Pat Metheny Real Book C Edition	$27.50
00252119	The Pat Metheny Real Book Bb Edition	$24.99
00240358	The Charlie Parker Real Book	$19.99
00118324	The Real Pop Book – Vol. 1	$35.00
00240331	The Bud Powell Real Book	$19.99
00240437	The Real R&B Book	$39.99
00240313	The Real Rock Book	$35.00
00240323	The Real Rock Book – Vol. 2	$35.00
00240359	The Real Tab Book	$32.50
00240317	The Real Worship Book	$29.99

THE REAL CHRISTMAS BOOK
00240306	C Edition	$32.50
00240345	Bb Edition	$32.50
00240346	Eb Edition	$32.50
00240347	Bass Clef Edition	$32.50
00240431	A-G CD Backing Tracks	$24.99
00240432	H-M CD Backing Tracks	$24.99
00240433	N-Y CD Backing Tracks	$24.99

THE REAL VOCAL BOOK
00240230	Volume 1 High Voice	$35.00
00240307	Volume 1 Low Voice	$35.00
00240231	Volume 2 High Voice	$35.00
00240308	Volume 2 Low Voice	$35.00
00240391	Volume 3 High Voice	$35.00
00240392	Volume 3 Low Voice	$35.00
00118318	Volume 4 High Voice	$35.00
00118319	Volume 4 Low Voice	$35.00

THE REAL BOOK – STAFF PAPER
00240327		$10.99

HOW TO PLAY FROM A REAL BOOK
00312097		$17.50

THE REAL BOOK – ENHANCED CHORDS
00151290		$29.99

Complete song lists online at www.halleonard.com

Prices, content, and availability subject to change without notice.

HAL•LEONARD®

0718